Nicolas Brasch

Why Is It So Loud?

and other questions about sound

CAMBRIDGE UNIVERSITY PRESS

How do
you measure
how loud
something is?

What is
sound?

Contents

- Questions about sound and noise 4
- Questions about sound and speed 8
- Questions about sound and reflection ... 10
- It's a fact 12
- Can you believe it? 14
- Who found out? 16
- It's quiz time! 20
- Glossary 24

Questions about sound and noise

Q: What is sound?

A: Sounds are **vibrations** that we can hear through air or water. As they travel, they change the pressure of the air or water and this makes the noise. Sound travels in waves. The **volume** depends on the height of the wave, and the **pitch** depends on the **frequency**.

sound waves

Q: How do our ears hear sound?

A: Our ears have three parts: the outer ear, the middle ear and the inner ear. The outer ear collects sound waves as they travel past and then sends them into the middle ear where they hit the ear drum and make vibrations. The vibrations move into the inner ear and then send messages to the brain.

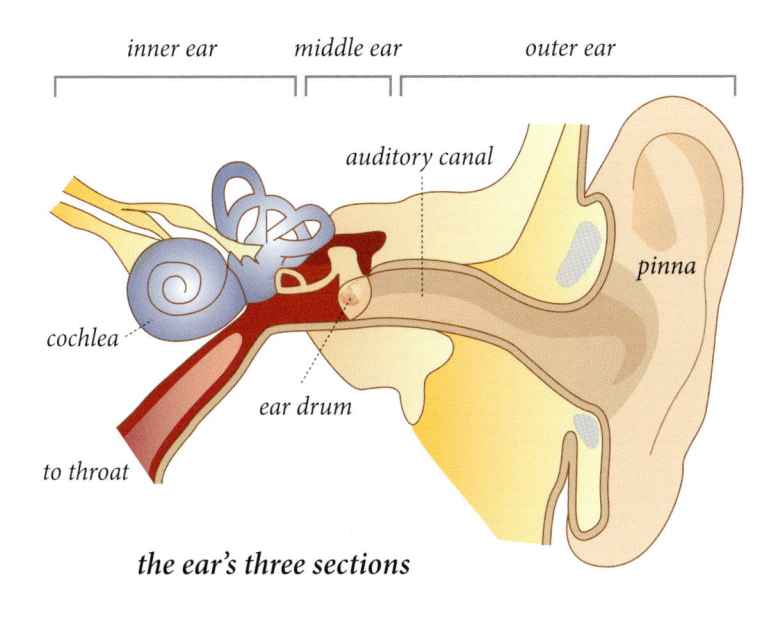

the ear's three sections

Q: How do you measure how loud something is?

A: We measure the volume of a sound in **decibels** (dB). There is a decibel scale which starts at 0, but the lowest sound that people can hear is 10. A jet aircraft overhead is about 130 on the decibel scale and the loudest rock bands in the world can make sounds that are about 150 dB.

air space

glass pane

Q: How does soundproofing work?

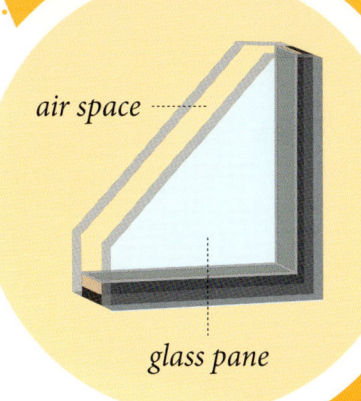

A: When we want to make a place quieter, we can use some objects to stop, or reduce, the noise reaching that place by **absorbing** some of the sound. For **soundproofing**, we use materials such as wool or foam that are very absorbent and can stop a lot of noise getting through.

Double glazing

We use double glazing to soundproof homes and offices. There are two panes of glass with a space in the middle. Most noise bounces off the first pane of glass. The air space absorbs any noise that gets through the first pane so it cannot get through the second pane of glass.

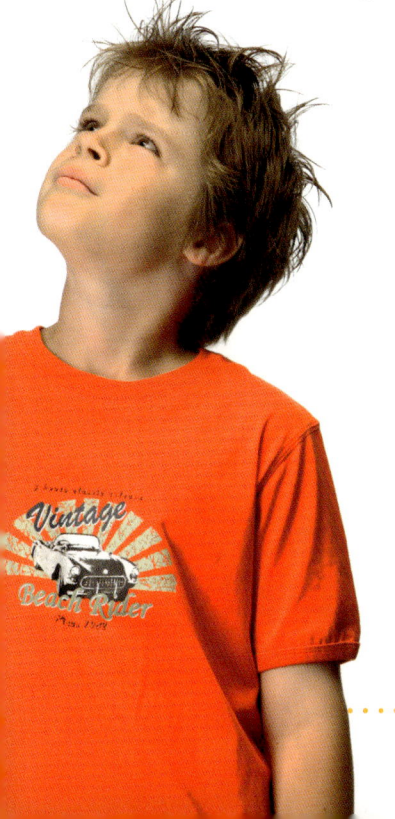

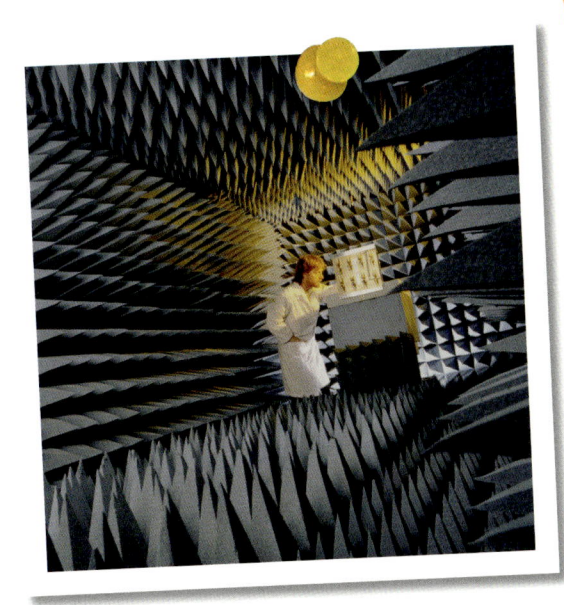

< *These soundproofing pyramids are made from carbon and other materials.*

Questions about sound and speed

Q: Why does the sound of a car change when it passes?

A: When a car is moving, the sound waves from the engine are further apart behind the car than they are in front of the car. This is because the movement of the car pushes the sound waves in front closer together and the sound waves behind are stretched out. When a car is coming towards you, you hear the high pitch from the sound waves at the front; then, when the car passes, you hear the lower pitch from the stretched out sound waves at the back. This is called the Doppler Effect.

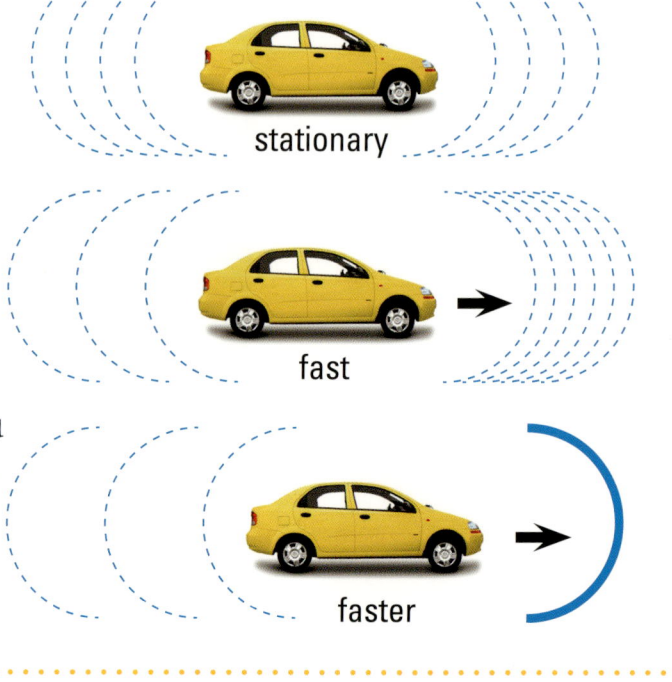

stationary

fast

faster

Q: Why do I hear thunder after I see lightning?

A: Lightning and thunder both happen at exactly the same time, but in fact it is the lightning that makes the thunder. You hear thunder after you see lightning because light travels much faster than sound. The speed of light is almost 300,000,000 metres (m) per second, but the speed of sound is only 340 m per second. That is why the light reaches our eyes before the sound reaches our ears.

Questions about sound and reflection

Q: Why are echoes not always clear?

A: Sound waves are like other energy waves, such as light. When they hit a surface, they bounce off it. They bounce best off surfaces that are hard and smooth, so when someone shouts in a cave, the sound bounces back off the walls very clearly. A soft surface, such as a pillow, absorbs sound waves so they cannot bounce back.

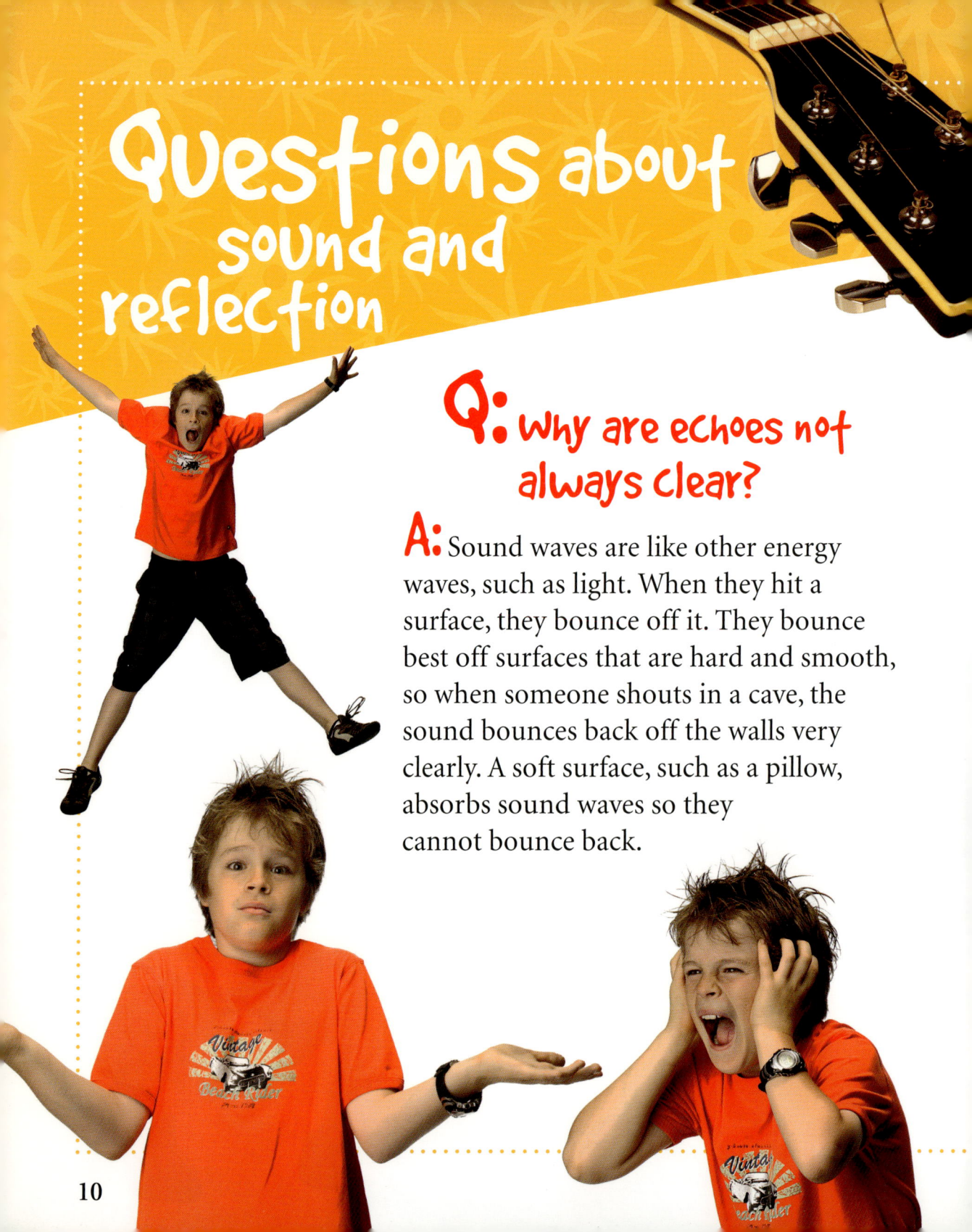

Q: What is the best design for a concert hall?

A: Some of the sound that you hear at a concert comes from the stage, but the walls and ceiling also **reflect** some sound waves. It is best when the walls and ceiling are hard and smooth, but people do not want to hear **echoes**, so it is good to also have soft, curved objects that can absorb some of the sound.

Lucerne Culture and Congress Centre, Lucerne, Switzerland

It's a fact

> Loudest animal sound
The blue whale makes the loudest sound. It can reach more than 180 dB and fish and other whales can hear it more than 800 kilometres (km) away.

> Loudest noise
The loudest noise humans have ever heard was the volcanic eruption of Krakatau in Indonesia in 1883. People could hear it more than 4,600 km away.

> A bat fact
Bats navigate, or find their way, by sound, not sight. They make noises and then listen to the echoes to know how close they are to objects.

> Sound to kill
The sound a blue whale makes is not just a way of communicating. The sound also stuns fish so they can't move and then the whale can catch them and eat them.

> **Sound and temperature**
Sound waves travel more slowly in cold weather than they do in warm weather.

> **Damage to the ears**
A noise of 140 dB or more can damage your hearing instantly. Listening to a noise of 110 dB for only one minute can be dangerous.

> **In one ear**
Sounds reach one ear just before they reach the other. This helps people to know which direction a sound is coming from.

dog
15Hz to 50,000Hz

human
20Hz to 20,000Hz

dolphin
120Hz to 170,000Hz

Sound and frequency
When sound waves are far apart (a low frequency) the pitch is low and when they are closer together (a high frequency) the pitch is high. We measure frequency in **hertz** (Hz). Humans can hear sounds up to 20,000 Hz, dogs can hear sounds up to 50,000 Hz and dolphins can hear sounds up to 170,000 Hz.

Can you believe it?

Breaking the sound barrier

When an aircraft travels faster than the speed of sound, it makes a huge 'boom'. This is because the aircraft pushes air away so fast that the waves of air crash into each other. The sound of a whip is made in the same way: the end of the whip is moving faster than the speed of sound.

Sound tracks

Sound engineers who work for TV, radio and films have to make a **soundtrack**. For example, if there are horses in the scene, they might make the beat of hooves and add splashing water as the horses run through a river.

Breaking a glass

A sound with a particular frequency and volume can make a crystal glass break. First the glass vibrates, and then, if the sound continues, the glass breaks. An opera singer who holds a high note for a long time can break a glass into many pieces.

Sound website for kids:

http://www.sciencetech.technomuses.ca/english/schoolzone/Info_Sound.cfm

Who found out?

Sound frequency: Galileo

Galileo Galilei (1564–1642) was an Italian physicist, astronomer and philosopher. He showed that the frequency of sound waves determined the pitch. He did this by scraping a chisel across a brass plate, producing a screech.

a chisel

The Doppler Effect: Christian Doppler

Austrian **physicist**, Christian Doppler (1803–1857) discovered that the distance between sound waves changes when they come from an object that is moving. He tested his idea by asking two trumpeters to play the same note at a train station. One trumpeter stood still, but the other was on a moving train. The sound made by the trumpeter who stood still stayed the same, but the sound made by the trumpeter on the moving train changed. This is now known as the Doppler Effect.

Inventor of the telephone: Alexander Graham Bell

The Scottish inventor, Alexander Graham Bell (1847–1922) probably invented the telephone. His mother was **hearing-impaired** and Bell was a teacher of people who were hearing-impaired.

In the 1870s, he began to find a way to **transmit** speech along wires. He changed the sound waves of speech into electrical signals that could travel along wires.

Phonograph: Edison

Thomas Alva Edison (1847–1931) was an American inventor who invented the phonograph, for recording and replaying sound. He called it a 'talking machine'. It was a revolving cylinder wrapped in tinfoil, with a sharp point pressed against it. He presented it in 1877 to the *Scientific American* magazine. The machine spoke to the editors, saying 'Good morning. How do you do? How do you like the phonograph?'

It's quiz time!

1 Which is the odd one out? Why?

1. middle ear, ear drum, outer ear, vibration

   _____

2. crystal glass, plastic bottle, metal bowl, paper cup

   _____

3. pillow, blanket, cave wall, clothes

   _____

4. volume, weight, frequency, hertz, decibels

   _____

2 Put these parts of the ear in the order that sound travels through them.

cochlea, pinna, auditory canal, ear drum

_____

3   Match the beginnings and endings of the sentences.

1. When an aircraft travels faster than the speed of sound, it makes a huge 'boom'

2. We usually know which direction a sound is coming from

3. Double glazing makes homes and offices quieter

4. Bats can find their way by sound, not sight,

a) because sounds reach one ear just before they reach the other.

b) because most noise bounces off the first pane of glass and the air space absorbs more noise.

c) because they can make noises and then listen to the echoes.

d) because the waves of air pushed away by the aircraft crash into each other.

4   Find 7 more words from the Factbook in the word search.

V	A	B	S	O	R	B	F	D	Q
I	O	B	G	G	Y	B	Q	E	S
B	D	L	G	G	P	I	T	C	H
R	Q	W	U	R	Z	X	V	I	E
A	H	K	L	M	H	Y	O	B	R
T	Z	Q	T	Y	E	J	P	E	T
I	Q	S	S	S	T	U	I	L	Z
O	M	Y	Y	U	Y	Q	G	S	G
N	A	V	I	G	A	T	E	C	B
S	O	U	N	D	P	R	O	O	F

Now use the words from the word search to complete the sentences. There is one word you will not need.

1. The volume of sound is measured in _____decibels_____ .

2. Materials such as wool or foam _____ a lot of noise.

3. Humans can hear sounds up to 20,000 _____ .

4. Bats _____ by sound, not sight.

5. _____ means the highness or lowness of a sound.

6. The _____ of a sound is how loud or quiet it is.

7. Sounds are _____ we hear through air or water.

5 Choose the correct words.

1. Alexander Graham Bell invented the (megaphone / telephone / microphone).

2. When sound waves hit a surface, they (dive / bounce / fall) off it.

3. The sound of a blue whale is the (loudest / highest / quickest) sound made by an animal.

4. Soundproofing materials (eat / absorb / reflect) a lot of noise.

Glossary

absorb: to soak up

decibels: units for measuring the loudness of sound

echo: a sound that we hear after it is reflected off a surface

frequency: how often a sound wave goes up and down per second

hearing-impaired: someone who cannot hear things very well

hertz: the unit we use to measure how often a sound wave goes up and down per second

physicist: someone who studies physics (the way things act and react)

pitch: how high or low a sound is

reflect: to send back sound when it hits a surface

soundproofing: a material that is used to reduce the amount of sound that can enter

soundtrack: the recorded music, speech and sound effects in a film

transmit: to send something from one place to another

vibrations: repeated movements back and forwards

volume: a measure of how loud a sound is